'All Shook Up'

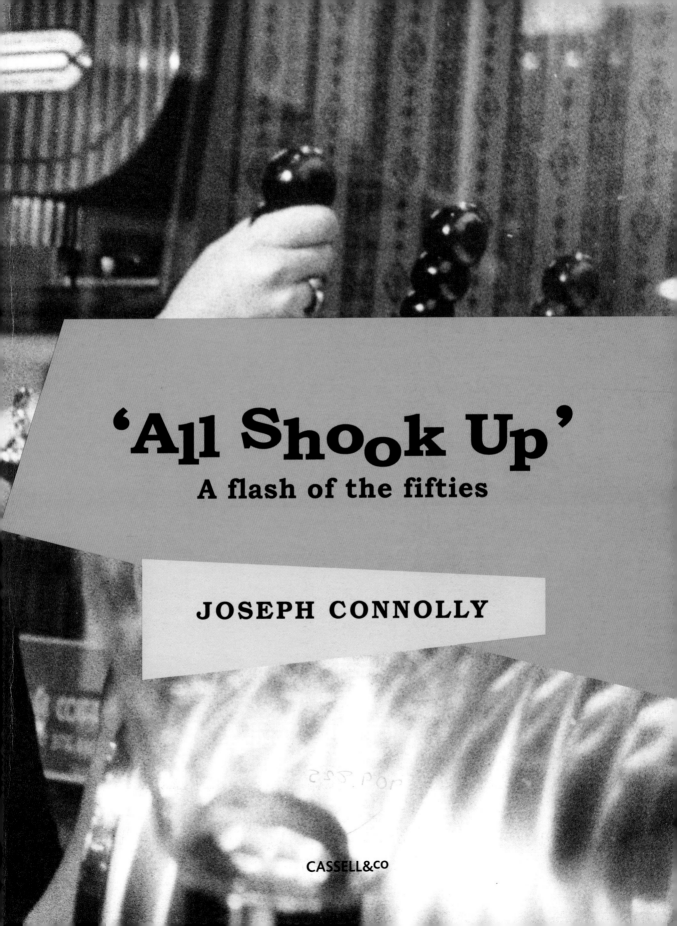

'All Shook Up'
A flash of the fifties

JOSEPH CONNOLLY

CASSELL&CO

This flash of the fifties is for Angela and Robert, whose decade it was.

First published in the United Kingdom in 2000 by Cassell & Co,
Wellington House, 125 Strand, London, WC2R 0BB

A CIP catalogue record for this book is available from the British Library

ISBN 0 304 35596 8

Printed and bound in Italy

Contents

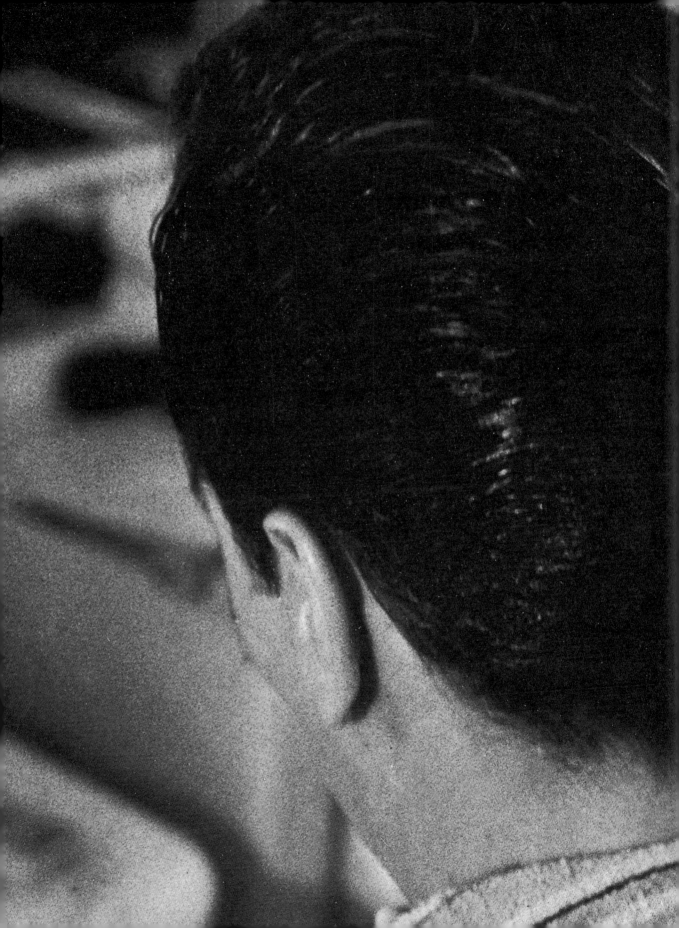

Introduction

Let the good times roll – that's what the song said. But for young people in the Fifties, these much vaunted good times did not seem to be that easy to get rolling. They had to be worked at and fought for: only then could they sweep you away.

Marilyn Monroe – one of the absolute symbols of America (and sex) in the Fifties ...

The Fifties era has recently been dubbed – by apparently sensible people who claim to have more than the first idea of what they're saying – 'Mid-Century Modern'. Well – we were, indisputably, half-way through the twentieth century, and the retrospective sight of beautiful, futuristic and now quite classic furniture of the period by such as Eames, Bertoia, Saarinen and Jacobsen would certainly seem to prop up the 'modern' end of things. But in Britain, this isn't, of course, remotely how it felt at the time. We thought of ourselves as not so much 'mid-century' as eternally 'post-war' – there was barely a day when that big little word 'war' did not arise in conversation in some or other context: not just memories of air-raid shelters, blackouts, blitzes and the Dunkirk Spirit, but the daily reality of torn asunder and war-scarred families, not to say the continued rationing of all manner of necessities, which hung around us like a shroud until 1954.

And were we, did we think, 'modern'? We *wanted* to be modern, desperately: any product marked as being in any way 'contemporary' had a pretty much guaranteed sale. But it all seemed rather hard and uphill work: to the young, it very much appeared that their parents' generation – while endlessly deploring the privations of the Forties – seemed nevertheless reluctant to let old habits die. To the young, the most glittering word of all was 'new' – but they were very aware that often even the concept of newness was viewed with tacit disapproval: colour and novelty, in the form of cars, clothes, curtains or carpets, were seen to be 'extravagant' – essentially unnecessary as well as, in some unspoken way, even dangerous. Older people appeared to be far more content while rubbing along, making do and mending, being grateful for small mercies – savouring each and every occasional modest treat, as if it could be their last.

And the young, of course, did not understand – and why should they? The war is *over*, right? So let's enjoy the times we've got. Hey – have you heard 'Heartbreak Hotel' by this way-out new guy, Elvis Presley? Have you seen his

... And here is the other one. No one had heard nor seen anything remotely like Elvis.

Catch them young: this lad seems more than happy to Watch *Without* Mother.

hair and the way he *moves*? And what about Marilyn Monroe? That voice and those eyes and that figure (barely contained in those *dresses* she wears)! Let's *go* with this – let's get a television. Why don't we? Dad? Mum? Let's get a telephone, yes? (I'm so damn sick of queuing in the rain outside those big red boxes and clonking in four great coppers and pressing button A and then waiting and then when they answer fooling around with sodding button B – and then if you mess it up, losing forever your four great coppers and what are the chances of having *another* load clanking about your person?)

But gradually – slowly, so slowly – the battle for modernity began to turn our way: a small black-and-white television took pride of place in the living-room corner, and opened up our eyes to more than we ever dreamed of. It wasn't just that *I Love Lucy*, say, was so quick and sharp and funny – but look at how ... *different* and *new* it is. Look at Lucy's polka dot dresses and look at the matching pair of sofas in her closely-carpeted split-level house and

(Opposite)
The quintessential TV show for all the family – Lucille Ball and Desi Arnaz in *I Love Lucy*: an eye-opener to style-starved Britain in more ways than one.

the (contemporary) art on the walls and those massive great chunky table lamps and that random stonework fireplace!

And nor did we want to go to chain store tea shops any more: we had discovered the new-style spotlit and Formica-clad coffee bar, its gleaming chromium Gaggia machines throatily disgorging cappuccinos into see-through Pyrex cups and saucers. Rock 'n' roll was suddenly a wild and throbbing alternative to *The Brains Trust* and the *Third Programme* and 'Clair de Lune' on the upright in the corner – and wherever rock was blaring was where we needed to be. We just had to get hold of 'new' by the throat, and shake it down for all it was worth.

We were not yet 'Mid-Century Modern': we were up to our eyes in 'Post-War Desperate' – and what we had to do was rip it up.

(Right) For a night out dancing, you just had to be young and fit, which was exactly how it should be. Rock the night away to a live band, or else make sure you're somewhere with that vital thing, a juke box (opposite).

1 Halfway to Paradise

Fifties childhood – a time when mothers no longer had to live in terror of bombs and blackouts, nor dread the conscription of their husbands and the evacuation of their children: after all those long, dark years of war, privation and enforced separations, the family unit was finally back in business.

Not that in the child's eye everything was Tizer and Roses (not by a long chalk), and neither was everything in the *garden* necessarily rosy (for a start, one was very likely to be dragooned into dragging a seized-up and utterly manual lawnmower over the tufty hillocks of moss and clover and dandelions that made up the typical Fifties back garden, and then gathering up the clippings and carting them off to the – groan, moan – compost

Boys couldn't skip, and girls were brilliant – which is why they seemed to spend their whole lives doing it.

heap). Because in those days children, by and large, did more or less as they were told (or at least had the nous to make it appear so), the main reason for this state of affairs being the universally acknowledged Great And Immutable Divide: it was very much a case of Them and Us. Parents, aunties and uncles, teachers, policemen and shopkeepers were not, you see, simply older and (maybe) wiser versions of ourselves (oh good heavens, no) but clearly emanated from *another and very distant planet*. And as for really *really* old people like grandparents and hairy-lipped and rancid honorary 'aunts', redolent of damp and decay and parma violets and whom you actually had to, oh yuck, *kiss* (in addition to other assorted truly incomprehensible weirdnesses such as nuns and men with beards) – well,

these self-evidently were nothing but very worrying branches of some even more mutant underworld altogether, and generally very much to be avoided – even if such defiance led to being sent straight up to one's room.

Which is another thing: one's room. Few were lucky enough to lay claim to a room of their very own (the designated 'box room' or sectioned-off after-thought often was polluted by such nuisances as younger brothers and piles of miscellaneous junk and broken furniture that one's father, rather pathetically, was convinced would one day 'come in handy'). But even assuming that one did indeed reign as lord over one's own domain, being forcedly detained there for some or other irrelevant culpability (watching Mister Pastry on the goggle-box, say, instead of being amazed by the wilful and lunatic con-trick that was algebra) was really not much fun at all. Today's child might run to more tech-nology than in those days would have been afforded to all the boffins at Cape

Quite an arresting sight – a cloudful of Fifties angels.

Canaveral, but nearly half a century ago we were talking linoleum floor (with maybe an offcut of heave-inducing Axminster close by the creaking bed frame) and if you ran to heating at all, it would be in the form of a horrible sort of clanking stove affair fuelled either by (pick one) Pink Paraffin or Esso Blue, each of them guaranteeing that you quickly turned a bilious and yellowish green as a result of the truly nauseous fumes.

Parents would strongly discourage the Sellotaping to the wall of pictures snipped from *Eagle* or *Girl*, working on the typically old-person-from-loony-bin logic that the peerless beauty of the actually disgusting beigy and flowery wallpaper would be irreparably marred *once the pictures were taken down*. There would be a Smith's or Westclox alarm clock (with a tick like a grossly amplified buffalo's heartbeat) in order to ensure that one was never ever late for school (being late for school, in terms of depravity, was viewed as being broadly along the lines of aggravated regicide). There might have been a shelf, upon which would lurk not very much at all, but possibly a few Jennings, William or Biggles books (if a boy) or else those eternal ramblings about big-eyed black horses and ballet shoes (if the other thing). And maybe a partially assembled Airfix Wellington bomber with all the big and easy bits done, and a lot of dust on the wing that keeps on falling off.

There would have been a single lightbulb dangling from an unravelling mauvish cloth-covered flex, fixed into the central ceiling rose: the bulb was shaded by something akin to a pagoda rooftop (again, beigy and flowery) and trimmed by a fringe that

An American scene that we could only wonder at. Why didn't *we* run to public fountains on every street corner?

would not have disgraced the sleeves of Roy Rogers' tunic. And the bulb itself would be either blindingly bright and stark, or else very dim indeed, depending upon the particular branch of madness towards which your father inclined. Later came James Bond in half-crown Pan paperbacks. An odd cove, 007 – why, when he easily could have had a hotel room all to himself, did he always want to bunk up with some *girl*? And this thing about his drinks being not stirred, but shaken: I tried it once with my Ovaltine and it all just went everywhere.

Leapfrog was great – everyone could do it except for the very fat kids, who got leapt over whether they liked it or not. And it was free!

Halfway to Paradise

But yes, despite or because of all this – we made our own fun. *Parents* didn't think so, of course: in their day, *they* had made their own fun, but naturally – oh yes, very much so. Back in 1066, or whenever it was, they were never happier than when given a stale cake to kick around or maybe a tea chest to sit in or a piece of lumber to chew. But *our* lot – the spoiled Fifties generation – well, in the words of our great and apparently thousand-year-old Prime Minister Harold Macmillan, we had never had it so good. And of course, in many ways, this was absolutely true. Girls, for instance, had skipping ropes. Girls just *loved* their skipping ropes, and giggling gaggles of them would take turns to gyrate the things faster and faster as some smarty-pants clever-clogs among their number would negotiate each revolution with ease and a carefree abandon. They didn't *just* have skipping ropes, girls, of course: they also had prams – Triang prams, complete with chrome wire wheels and real, bouncy and leather-girt suspension and a fold-

The girls are thinking 'Don't We Look Lovely?' And the solitary boy is wishing he were dead.

This is more like it –
a street-level ambush
by a descendant of
Sitting Bull, newly
in possession of
The Cisco Kid's
sixshooter (and he's
not afraid to use it).

away and elasticated hood and a little shiny Rayon quilt and a big pink stiff-limbed vinyl dolly with a Diana Dors-coloured spark-making Toni home perm riveted into its skull in grudging and gappy chunks. And this doll would be called Elizabeth and the mummy-girl would love it more than anything in the whole wide world, despite the fact that you would often see it face down under the table for days on end, the odd chubby leg occasionally turning up in the sweet drawer, or floating helplessly in the bath amid the swirling residue of Matey bubbles.

(Previous pages)
When schoolboys looked like schoolboys – here let loose amid the unspeakable joys of the fabulous corner sweetshop.

What we all adored was that rare and precious thing – television. Television was our prize – our tantalisingly brief but justly earned reward for endlessly enduring not just school but school caps and horribly chafing and draughty short trousers and circulation-arresting garters wrapped into itchy stockings and Start-Rite lace-ups and Clark's white crepe-soled sandals (the only good bit here being when you examined the bones in your feet, ghostly green via the X-Ray machine in the shop, the cumulative effects of which one day will probably annihilate us all) and dancing lessons and piano lessons (Where is middle C? Who among us actually *cares*?) and school dinners and cod liver oil when you're not even poorly (illness generally being acceptable only due to missing lessons and the existence of Lucozade) and washing bits that nobody sees and combing one's hair *all the way round* and finishing up all one's lovely spinach (all efforts to explain that in fact you don't actually *want* to grow up to be a deformed and unintelligible sailor with a seven-foot girlfriend invariably falling on deaf ears and a quite closed mind).

But television was our new and special friend – from the early delights of (watching with mother) Andy Pandy (and never mind that he always seemed to be saying 'goodbye') and The Flowerpot Men (God alone knew what *they* were saying), the fabulous Muffin the Mule (with strings like hawsers) and the anarchic puppet Sooty – who would first drench and then hit with a hammer one of *Them*, an oldie: bliss. Then there was the very English innocence of Robin Hood (forever riding through that glen) before the flood of real excitement – American stuff. American children, we divined early on, were different and much to be envied. They played in the spray of burst street hydrants (whatever they were). Their clothes and toys were cooler and scaled-down versions of the real and glitzy grown-up thing – and they had cowboys! With guns! The Lone Ranger with his mask and his Tonto (to say nothing of the William Tell Overture) – a silver gun with silver bullets (they gave away grey plastic ones in Puffed Wheat but I only got one before they changed the offer, so I switched to Corn Flakes and got baking powder-fuelled submarines instead). And then there was Hawkeye with twitface Chingachgook and The Cisco Kid, Hopalong Cassidy and Roy

(Overleaf)
Every schoolchild's friend: the perpetual ineptitude of Norman Wisdom on screen truly struck a chord.

Rogers (horses called Diablo, Topper and Trigger, respectively) as well as those two dogs Lassie and Rin Tin Tin, either of which would have sailed like a breeze through anything the 11-Plus could have thrown at them. At the *pictures*, of course (Wall's tubs and choc ices and the terror when the lights went down of never again seeing your seat or your mummy), there was no one to touch Norman Wisdom – because he was an idiot, and so one saw his point of view.

And of course we knew that life was good. How could it not be when in the corner sweetshop you could get chews at four a penny and pygmies for a

The Americans were different. Which ragtop limo should this shrunken Sinatra select? Decisions, decisions …

An understated Roy
Rogers, serenading
Trigger (Dale Evans
always did come a
very poor second).

(Opposite)
This little girl is
justly thrilled to bits
to be astride a giant
Muffin the Mule,
alongside the gawky
creature's creator,
Annette Mills.

halfpenny each (bite their heads off first) and liquorice pipes with the red smoulder of hundreds and thousands and coconut tobacco and Barratt's sweet cigarettes (a plague upon your 'candy wands') and colour-changing gobstoppers and Rowntree's Fruit Gums, Jamboree Bags, Mars bars, Smarties (never mind Lulu – buy some for *me*!), Fry's Chocolate Cream and Cadbury's, oh – just *anything*. Not to mention the *Beano* and the *Dandy* and Matchbox toys and Dinkies and Corgis – I-Spy books, Meccano, soldiers, water pistols, yo-yos and Post Office sets (Pedigree dolls and hula hoops for the girls – tricky, these, as hips were not quite yet on the agenda).

The great diversion, of course, was a train set – Hornby Dublo or Triang 'oo gauge', for preference – boasting, if you were lucky, perfectly miniaturised tankers with the liveries of Shell or Esso emblazoned on their flanks, and open wagons marked Coalite. If one's father wasn't interested in this sort of thing (there are such men) then it is likely that all one ran to was an oval track, maybe a platform and possibly some dusty fencing cobbled up out of

Here is the idealised version: television underpinning the family unit.

(Opposite) **More the reality. How can Mum and Dad want to be in the boring old garden when Robin Hood's on? Beings from another planet.**

corrugated cardboard and daubed a muddy green with Rowney's poster paint. If this *was* the old man's sort of thing, though, we could be talking about a re-creation of Crewe meets Clapham Junction – in which case, of course, one wouldn't get a look in.

And to round it all off, what about a slap-up feed of Bird's Eye fish fingers or beefburgers with crinkle-cut chips (the real thing – a Wimpy – only sometimes on birthdays) followed by Carnation milk swamping Libby's fruit cocktail (leave the half cherries till last), all helped down by a generous measure of R. White's Cream Soda? Then there would be a bath, shivering on one's knees while asking God to please bless both Mummy and Daddy, and then getting tucked in warm and tight for the night.

And of course we knew that life was good.

Week ending September 14 1957 — *Every Wednesday Fourpence*

JOHN BULL

Begins inside: THE MASK
Tempestuous new novel by

STUART CLOETE

Transvaal—where pioneers battled against a witchdoctor and two girls fought for the love of an adventurer

---

THE MAN WHO KNOWS WHICH HATS SUIT WOMEN

2 It's Only
Make Believe

Nowadays it's called 'taking in a movie'; back in the Fifties, one went to the pictures, and each and every time it was something of an event. Everyone from schoolchildren to grannies flocked to the intimate twilight of the Odeon stalls and circles, and settled down to living out their own sweet dreams.

Just as a visit to a restaurant is never solely about the food and drink, so a trip to the cinema always meant more than just the quality of the film on offer: what we had here was an evening out – or, even naughtier, a stolen sunlit afternoon to squander in the welcoming darkness. Meeting in the foyer was very much part of the ritual, as was a prior scanning of the listings in a local or evening paper – and, if a couple was involved, this could usually be relied upon to generate a fairly heated debate: *he* might want to see something stern

Queuing – and checking the paper for what's on next week – was almost as much fun as the film. If it wasn't raining.

Text visible within the image: AIR TIDY? · HAVED? · COLLAR CLEAN? · TIE NEAT? · UNIFORM PRESSED & CLEAN? · HANDS CLEAN?

This is how cinema staff were expected to look at all times. Haven't we come a long way?

and manly like *High Noon*, where *she* might incline to romantic escapism – something on the lines of *The King and I*, say – and very often a compromise was struck: the neither-one-thing-nor-the-otherness of *Genevieve*, for instance, which no one really ever wanted to watch in the first place.

Sometimes – and usually when it was raining – the amber warmth of the foyer was not a viable option, and queuing the length of the cinema's blustery flank was the order of the day (for reasons, actually, that eluded just everyone, but neverthe-less queue we did – for the British have never been slouches when it comes to

The American dream – an open-topped car, and an open-topped movie house.

patiently and silently standing in line and occasionally shuffling forward under the dangled incentive of some half-promised and dubious reward). And the very queuing system itself – as with most branches of ceremony and ritual that riddled the Fifties – was all about status and class, real or implied, the pecking order proudly on display for all to see plainly, and draw their own conclusions: the longest queues were always for the cheapest seats – whereas if you'd made up your mind to push out the boat and treat your oh-so-lucky girlfriend to a central seat in the front of the dress circle, you could normally expect to just sweep past the huddled and snuffling masses, plank down your eight-and-six (yikes – that's seventeen shillings for the pair of us, and I promised her a raspberry Mivvi in the interval and a Wimpy and chips later on: I just hope she's grateful) and pausing only to pick up a rattling carton of Payne's Poppets or Sun-Pat Chocolate Covered Raisins at the 'kiosk' (another two bob gone west), swan up the thickly carpeted treads of the

Romantic, or what?
The film was practically
an irrelevance.

The stunning luminosity of Marilyn clearly has the man behind her in thrall. Laurence Olivier, on the left, is apparently – and not for the first time – wishing he were elsewhere.

Grand Staircase, and thrill to the anticipation that always gripped you. In the unnecessarily vast and opulent lounge upstairs (where you'd whisper, even if the nearest people were twenty yards distant, whispering also) you would do your level best to block out the muffled final exchanges of the current screening, and visibly perk up as the closing music swelled to its inevitable climax – and soon the rumble of filmgoers and the smacking back of burgundy velvet seats would be overtaken by the emerging hordes themselves – smug in their superiority over you, because *they* had seen the film (could tell you the twists and yawn at the dull bits) and you were just a rookie.

And you certainly did get value for money: not just the main event, but that much-lamented thing – a B-movie, in addition to *Look at Life*, a brief and

merry showcase for individual aspects of life in Britain – plus, the great Pearl &
Dean adverts ('Salesgirls will visit all parts of the theatre' – great: it's Kia Ora
and Fruit Parfait time!) as well as the all-important trailers for the following
week's programme, when we'd all be sure to come back. Sometimes, even a
Pathé newsreel was thrown in for good measure. Also (Quick! Let's get out!)
the National Anthem.

At the smarter cinemas, the staff were splendidly turned out and endlessly
inspected throughout the day by unsmiling managers. The usherettes with those
rather exciting red-cowled torches would not have disgraced the Wrens. Very
often, the film on offer would, of course, be American – and once again we
would be afforded this chink of light shed upon so huge and alien a world. If

**Tony Curtis, despite
his best efforts, is not
as lovely as Marilyn.**

It's Only Make Believe

Diana Dors ushers some much-needed beauty into dull old Venice. Her £150 mink bikini *(below)* seems an eminently practical accessory – as does her open-topped pink Cadillac *(opposite)*, in which she was driven around during the Cannes Film Festival of 1956.

Rock Hudson and Doris Day, say, were acting as a couple who were going to the movies, did you see them arguing over the *Evening Standard* and donning slate-grey Pakamacs (Doris's hairdo well protected by an unfolded concertina of transparent Polythene, tied neatly in a bow beneath her chinny-chin-chin) and standing in a queue for the two-and-fours? You did not. You saw them wearing colours like Caribbean turquoise, blush pink, pillar box red and banana yellow (and that was just Rock) – colours that in Britain were only ever glimpsed fleetingly in a quarter of Dolly Mixtures, and certainly not on the racks of C&A or Burton, where mid-grey, navy and various hues with their roots in gruel still held sway over the affections of the Great British public. And would the gaily bedecked Rock and Doris climb to the top of the 38 bus because they fancied, respectively, a Falcon pipeful of Three Nuns and a cork-tipped Craven 'A'? No – they'd slither across the not just piped leather but deep lavender bench seat of their huge and chromey convertible Buick, Oldsmobile, Chevrolet, Cadillac or Pontiac (even the words could trigger off a fever), light up a couple of Luckies with a Zippo and *cruise* there. Not just to the entrance of the cinema, though – oh no: right up to the

Doris Day – about as lipsmackingly wholesome as they come. Dontcha just love her?

(Opposite) **What can you say about Brigitte Bardot that isn't already so very clear from this photograph? Except that she really ought to get out of those wet clothes of hers.**

screen itself! And there they would sit, perchance to smooch – their in-car speaker hooked up over the windshield – grabbing alternate fistfuls of popcorn from a vast cardboard bucket – all beneath an eternal indigo canopy, stuck with bright white Hollywood stars (a far cry from a bag of nuts in the front stalls of the Roxy, I think you'll readily agree).

Blondes like Doris Day were very big news. Not, of course, that there was *actually* a blonde remotely like Doris Day – she was a one-off, and had neatly cornered the market in wholesomeness and feistiness and being a good wife and mother and the original virgin all at the same time. The blonde to end all blondes, though, was of course the sainted Marilyn Monroe. Marilyn came to be *the* quintessential icon of Fifties America – and which of us will ever forget the billowing white halter-neck dress in *The Seven Year Itch* or the shoulderless number in *Bus Stop* or the fringed and shimmery little nothing she wore as the irresistible Sugar in *Some Like It Hot* (where she amply demonstrated, with the help of Tony Curtis and Jack Lemmon in drag, that it took more than lipstick, powder and paint to make up a credible woman)? Dear Marilyn – a devil to work with, apparently, but simply magical up there on the screen. By way of an example of both these truths, the director of *Some Like It Hot*, Billy Wilder, tells of the endless takes where Marilyn was supposed to husk seductively through the panels of a door 'It's me – Sugar'. As the crew looked on in amazement, she came out with every sort of variation, time and time again ('It's Sugar – Me'; 'Me Sugar – It') until after about Take 52, Wilder – sensing the tension on set – drew her aside and told her it was OK, not to worry about it. She looked at him wide-eyed – as only Marilyn could do – and said 'Worry about what?' And of course, everyone forgave her, and the printed version was flawless. Laurence Olivier, during the filming of *The Prince and the Showgirl*,

Grace Kelly, the soon-to-be princess, looking queenly – and *(opposite)* **Hitchcock the Master, who cast her as often as he could, but never, to his profound regret, across the couch.**

reportedly came close to murdering her, but never mind.

Although never even close to the Marilyn league, Britain could boast its own home-grown 'blonde bomb-shells', as they were rather touchingly called, pre-eminent among them being Diana Dors (née Fluck). She may have been celebrated for her armour-plated and gravity-defying twin Zeppelin bosom (in common with another bombshell, Sabrina, who was, um – well actually no one was ever quite sure what on earth Sabrina was) but – as she proved in the 1956 film *Yield to the Night*, based loosely on the Ruth Ellis murder case and her subsequent hanging – Diana Dors was actually a very useful actress. Predictably, though, she was far more regularly cast as the vacuous glamour – a fate never suffered by that most gorgeous embodiment of sex ever to hit the silver screen, Brigitte Bardot. Bardot – unlike many other blondes of the period – was never perceived to be stupid; maybe we were all stunned by not just her sensational presence but also her cleverness in being so very good at French. Of course, with all that pulchritude coming full at you, there was no time to bother with the subtitles in such cool and Gallic eye-openers as Roger Vadim's 1956 effort *And God Created Woman* (which was, wasn't it – when you come to think about it – just as well?).

Audrey Hepburn
blending very well
into the bohemian
Paris scene. It was
1957, and she was
over there filming
the dance sequences
for *Funny Face*
with veteran genius
Fred Astaire.

A blonde of a very different order was Grace Kelly – the so-called 'ice goddess', whatever that means, who went on to become a real live princess and, not too long after, a very dead one. The great Alfred Hitchcock would have cast her in every single film he made, had she been available, but was forced to content himself with just three fine examples: *Dial M for Murder*, *Rear Window* and *To Catch a Thief* (opposite Ray Milland, James Stewart and Cary Grant, respectively). Hitchcock had a thing for blondes in general, and Kelly in particular – who wasn't averse to having flings, reportedly, with any number of

Elizabeth Taylor –
not screen testing
for Hitchcock's
The Birds, but in
Trafalgar Square
in 1957 (maybe
having a good time,
maybe not).

leading men and directors, but she drew the line at not just lowlife such as writers but, distressingly for the Master, Hitch himself.

Not that blondes had *all* the fun – the head-on voluptuousness of violet-eyed Elizabeth Taylor (at her most smoulderingly beautiful in *Cat on a Hot Tin Roof*, with Paul Newman, in 1958) was hardly to be ignored, and nor were the uniquely gamine charms of Audrey Hepburn – then as now, admired more by women, maybe, than by men. And *talking* of men – the female filmgoer really was rather spoilt for choice in terms of heroes: every taste was catered for – everyone from Laurence Olivier to Marlon Brando was yours for the price of a seat in the stalls: Montgomery Clift, Gene Kelly, Orson Welles, Yul Brynner, Charlton Heston – particularly splendid in *Ben Hur*, the doyen of all those Roman and Biblical epics with American accents – Richard Burton, Henry

Tony Curtis –
delighted to be
wearing trousers
again – with just a
few very close
sycophants, hanging
on his every quip.

Fonda, Gary Cooper, James Stewart, John Wayne, Cary Grant, Kirk Douglas, Gregory Peck, James Dean, Burt Lancaster ... God, they really knew how to make film stars, in those days.

In contrast to the Hollywood mega-films, British cinema was edging gently into its most innovative phase – groundbreaking films such as *Look Back in Anger* and *Room at the Top* were among the more thoughtful, while for those of a more lighthearted disposition there was always the wonderful/ghastly (tick one) *Carry On Sergeant*, the 1958 forerunner for the wildly successful and apparently never-ending string of wacky comic capers, all of them – very gratifyingly for the British, this – more or less identical.

Tell you what – I'll meet you Friday, in the foyer of the Gaumont, just inside the door: seven o'clock suit you? I'll be dapper in my new John Collier suit, a nice Van Heusen drip-dry and an off-white shortie mac; if you're good, I'll go halves with my Mint Chocs. OK? And we'll have a cappuccino later. OK? Yes? Right then – it's a date.

(Opposite) **While we were nursing a carton of Kia Ora orange, the Americans were doing it bigger and better.**

At the movies
entertainment and refreshment go hand in hand

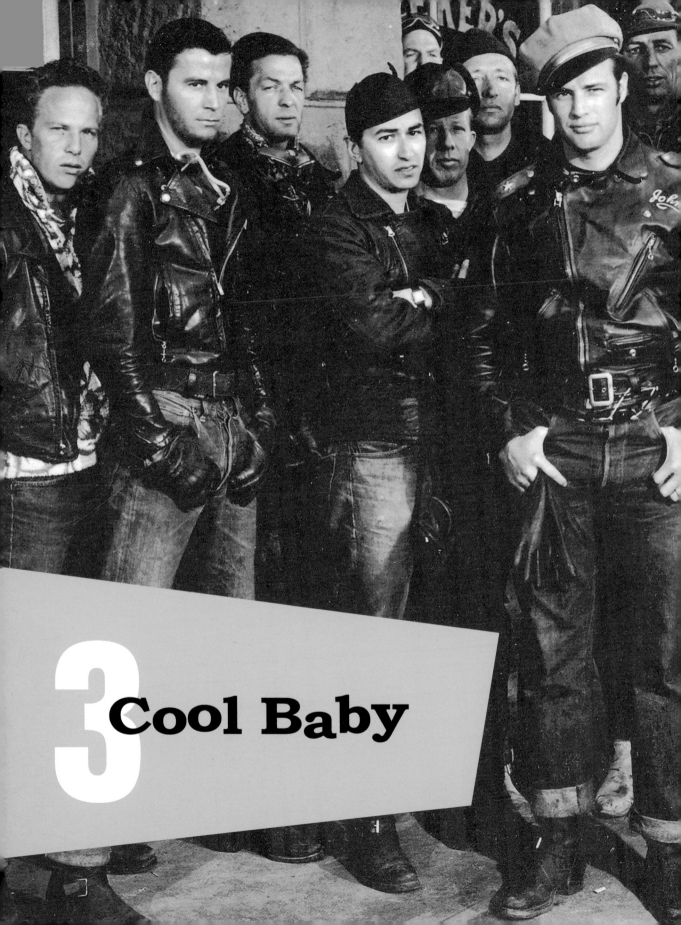

3 Cool Baby

Cool Baby

It has always been one of the driving forces of teenagedom – to shrug off the mantle of gawkiness and cloak oneself instead in top-to-bottom *cool*. In the Fifties, there were more ways than ever to achieve this end, every one of which was uniformly deplored by the oldies – proof indeed that one had got it right.

America kicked the whole thing off – if only because to be cool was to be loose-limbed and easy, and the US of A appeared to all of us just about the most casual and laid-back place on earth. We had glimpsed the seeds of it in black-and-white war films, where British officers would be very literally tightly buttoned-up and utterly correct, while the eager Tommies beneath them seemed to be not so much at ease in their battledress as ungainly – and, no doubt, with the weight of all that khaki wool and the heft of those terrible boots, distinctly hot and bothered on the top of it. The GI, however, was a different animal – a prowler. The strap on his helmet would always hang loose, three-day stubble seemed mandatory, and from his undone breast pocket he would freely dispense an endless supply of full-strength untipped Camels and Wrigley's Spearmint Gum; full-scale US generals with five silver stars studding their gleaming bullet helmets sported flash-white cravats and Ray-Ban Aviators and just how faint-makingly cool was that?

The US army also supplied the lower ranks with 'fatigues' – tough and no-nonsense workwear strong enough to deal with the backbreaking chores in which the enlisted men always seemed to be engaged, while not singlehandedly bringing Hitler to his knees. T-shirts – so-called because of their shape when pressed out flat – had their origins as US army singlets (I would say vests, but Americans think that vests are waistcoats, just as they imagine pants to be

trousers – it's a minefield out there) to be worn beneath collared shirts and dogtags. By the Fifties, many young manual workers had adopted the T-shirt and dumped the topwear, while teaming it with industrial strength and stiff-as-a-board indigo top-stitched and riveted denim – not that much changed from the original workwear of the 1890s, designed and marketed by Levi Strauss with gold prospectors and other hardworking and penniless optimists in mind. Young kids working their way through college by means of jerking soda, parking cars and pumping gas soon started wearing a modified version, and close on the heels of that – from amid the haze of gasoline vapour and the

(Previous pages)
Marlon Brando – the coolest of cool in *The Wild One* and *(above)* the original and unaffected workwear that inspired a generation. These guys are cool too, give or take an Easter bonnet.

Easy to see how James Dean became an icon in his own (brief) lifetime. Here – with Corey Allen in *Rebel Without a Cause* – he is seen with just everything: the hair, the cigarette and that knowing leer that said 'lock up your daughters'.

throbbing of engines – there emerged the stylised, scowling and barely articulate icon Marlon Brando in the film *The Wild One* (1954, but frequently banned all over the place mainly, it seems, because the unruly and amoral gang are seen to get away with it). James Dean bolstered the image, as did, of course, the King: Elvis Presley in the days before Colonel Parker and the Military had jointly cleaned him up some, and that down-home Memphis boy was still just dripping with sex and hair grease, and working that pelvis to the

Elvis when he was
still a regular work-
booted, denim-clad
tough guy (maybe
taking an inventory
of his current crop
of pets).

beat of the drum like a mean and horny lowdown hound dog. The mix by
now was already a potent one: add to it the thick short black zipped biker's
leather jacket and what you had was volatile. Throw in the Harley Davidson
and we are all – averred the old, the scared and the frankly appalled – sitting
astride a jerry-built time bomb, primed to detonate at just any time at all and
blast us all to hell and damnation. All of which, so far as the kids were concerned, was totally cool.

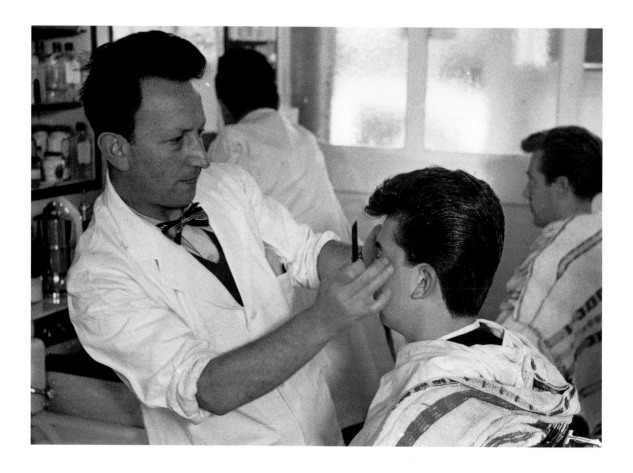

**Mr Rose himself –
the self-styled
creator of the quiff –
caught in the act
of being a slave
to his art.**

Not that this was the sole direction for American youth, disaffected or otherwise. Most college boys and girls – as memorably depicted in the *Archie* comics – would project a far less threatening image, but they too seemed very easy and enviably confident in their everyday duds: the now ubiquitous T-shirt (but also button-down Oxfords), chinos, sneakers and those very puzzling baseball jackets – thick, zippered and brightly coloured boxcloth displaying all manner of indecipherable letters and numbers writ large like a hoarding, and those seemingly padded leather sleeves with elasticated cuffs: we could but stare and wonder. Girls seemed happy and carefree with their jaunty pony tails, twin sets, pencil skirts, Capri pants, bobby sox, ballet pumps and an abundance of gingham, puffed out by petticoats – *Youth* was the message here. The more vampish and sophisticated look for girls remained the preserve of the more fashion-conscious corners of the Continent

– France and Italy, most notably, as well as, somewhat surprisingly, Britain (and more of this later).

For young men in this country, meanwhile, all sorts of strange new things were, for the first time in just ages, at last and finally beginning to happen – yes, a whole new look had suddenly emerged. Well … let's qualify that: for *some* young men, anyway, this was true … and the look itself, um – wasn't *actually* very new at all: the long-line drape jacket, often with a velvet collar, and slimline trousers all dated back to the Edwardian era – which is why these oh-so-cool dandies who sported the style came quickly to be dubbed with the monicker 'Teddy Boys'. Initially this term carried with it a degree of indulgence,

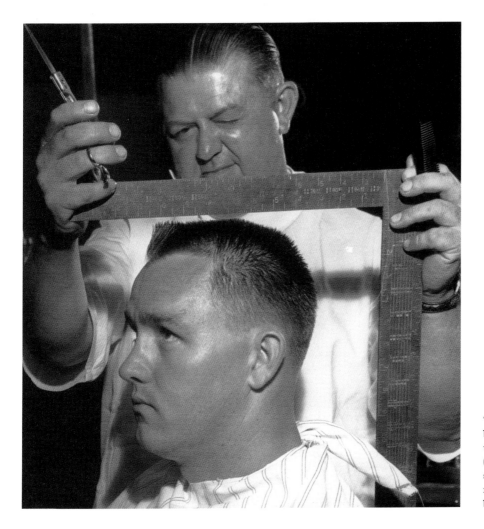

The American buzz-cut had to stand up and be counted (while leaving the sides to appear as if recently grazed upon by starving goats).

Cool, or what? The very well turned out Teddy Boys here took the whole thing very seriously indeed, despite their jaunty disposition. Our nonchalant friend on the right *(opposite)*, however, is a graduate of approved schools, Borstal and prison.

if not outright affection, but then the 'Teds' became associated with street crime and gang rivalry – as partially mimicked from the new musical *West Side Story* – whereupon they became a synonym for delinquency, oikdom, spivvery, violence and general all-round bad egginess.

And now the matter of class, once more, rears its brilliantined head. The extremes of fashion were most keenly followed by what were then unflinchingly termed 'the working classes'; the middle classes, very largely, had to wait until

Cool Baby

As these shots show, all you had to do was get the threads, meet your mates, talk the talk and walk the walk. The dark side here, though, is that these young men had just appeared on charges arising out of the infamous Notting Hill race riots of 1958.

the Sixties for their own liberation, while the upper classes were still too busy living out whole chapters from *Brideshead Revisited* and gently breaking in their grandfather's dinner jacket (much as many of them continue to do to this day and, rather endearingly, will *continue* so to do well into the foreseeable future ... or, let's face it, unto eternity). Just as in the United States, where the clean-cut all-American guy would be proud of his precision-engineered *en brosse* buzz-cut (sometimes called the crew cut) or else favour maybe a simple side-parted college boy crop, so in Britain the old ways generally prevailed. Undergraduates and those in work would more or less stick to whatever varia-

tion on a short-back-and-sides they were dumped with at school, give or take a gouging of Vaseline, while their clothes would incline towards nondescript flannels, corduroys, Harris Tweed jackets, checked shirts and just *maybe* tan suede shoes, or otherwise good old brogues. In other words – in the eyes of the Jack-the-Lad kids with a few quid to burn – as big a drag as their sodding parents: look, it ain't the job of any self-respecting teenager, mate, to come across like an unwrinkled version of his boring old man: you had to be *different* – lead the way; you had to have respect on the street; let's be clear, here – you simply just had to be *cool*.

Modern young men in an all-but-vanished setting: the corner shop and a cobbled street, pretty much free of cars and parking.

The less structured
approach: this chorus
line of groovy guys
and chicks had been
hand-plucked from
the streets of Soho
by Lionel Bart to
lend authenticity
to his 1959 musical
*Fings Ain't Wot They
Used to Be.*

Let us start at the top, with the quiff. Britain actually lays claim to having invented this, by way of an East End hairdresser known simply as Mr Rose. As early as 1954 he had piled up his own Barnet high on his head, encouraged just the hint of sideburn to creep down past his ears, and finally had swept back the sides into the perfectly barbered and collar-length back so that these two wings formed themselves into the legendary 'duck's arse' (the expression quickly cleaned up by means of the acronym DA, leading many of us to be puzzled over a period of years as to the connection between a Teddy Boy's haircut and some distantly heard-of American lawman). Anyway, before long queues were forming outside Mr Rose's establishment and the quiff took flight, as it were – some more adventurous versions pressing into service the inner cardboard tube of a roll of hard and unforgiving Bronco toilet paper to act as an internal and impromptu scaffold for the resulting great and awesome, glorious overhang. (Teds, it will be seen, could never wear hats and nor, for equally evident reasons, could they venture out in the rain: collapsed quiffs and soggy bog rolls are no good to man nor beast, and there never was anything remotely cool about a brolly.)

The all-important threads were initially knocked up by bemused but supportive East End tailors – the overstated opulence of the lapelled, covered-buttoned waistcoat being particularly prized – and all sorts of variations on the theme were made possible by way of 'bootlace' ties, dicky-bows and stick-pinned cravats. Drainpipe trousers ended an inch or so above the shoes – buck-led slip-ons, for preference, either polished as glossily as a blackcurrant Rowntree's Fruit Gum, or else round-toed and suede, with a thick crepe sole (the much-loved 'brothel-creeper' – and into the origins of this expression, no

Rumpled and angry intellectual chic, as exemplified by Kenneth Haigh on stage at the Royal Court in John Osborne's *Look Back in Anger*, in 1956.

(Above) **Like, beatnik and bohemian cool, daddio – featuring the much-to-be-desired mouth-dangled cigarette. (Opposite) An ad for a very stylish brand – very big in the Fifties, despite the Art Deco pack.**

one really cared to delve); mauve socks, orange socks, white socks – any coloured socks, really, so long as they contrasted vibrantly with everything else on show and were plainly visible as their cock-of-the-walk wearer strutted on down the centre of the street – usually, it must be said, as part of a pack: these young men were daring pioneers, and one on his own was vulnerable to catcalls, at best, it not proffered violence. Some of them were into it just for the kit and the kicks; others carried knives (always, they insisted, to deflect any trouble and never, of course, with the intent of causing it).

While the pure and extreme Teddy Boy look remained in place (the self-same guys, indeed, more than forty years on are still displaying the duds with pride, only the quiffs having suffered in the meantime) a diluted version soon filtered down to the high street: John Collier ('The Window To Watch'), Burton, Cecil Gee and shoe chains such as Freeman, Hardy & Willis were collectively responsible for a less self-conscious and easier street-style, while Brylcreem did its bit to help make painstakingly hand-formed quiffs modelled vaguely on that of our very own living doll, Cliff Richard, at least a possibility, if not quite a going concern. T-shirts (sometimes under a 'Sloppy Joe' sweater) and denim jeans were everywhere (Levi's and Wrangler the most sought-after brands) and such unlikely standbys as Woolworth were found to stock a really neat black canvas and white rubber-toed lace-up ... well, it *wasn't* a plimsoll, it really wasn't – because it came up over your ankle, see,

du MAURIER
FILTERED FOR FLAVOUR

and they were only seven-and-eleven and they looked just great. Zip-front windcheaters (and I didn't know then that that's how you spelt it), Clark's pale suede Desert Boots and soft-soled moccasins all made their mark – as did matching 'tie-and-hank sets', with optional tie-tack, for when you went Up West, or else took your bird down the Palais. (One very curious take on the craze for visible pocket handkerchiefs was a cardboard rectangle, and stapled to the top of it three or five cloth points in the form of chunks of Toblerone: you picked a pattern, trimmed the card to fit, and away you went. These cost sixpence, were sold out of a suitcase, and there is no record of the consequences should some distraught and mascara-smudged woman have tugged it out of your pocket, wholly intent on a full-blown weep, swiftly followed by two good honks of the horn.)

Another variation on the scene was the rather more 'high-brow' look, for those who believed in 'The Angry Young Men' and favoured the lasting pleasures of Kingsley Amis's *Lucky Jim* or John Braine's *Room at the Top* in Penguin, or John Osborne at the Royal Court, over the more transient if immediate delights of The Avons's 'Seven Little Girls Sitting in the Back Seat Huggin' and A-kissin with Fred'. A parallel (they called it 'beatnik') strain was palpable in America (their gods being 'method acting' à la Brando, and the new Beat poets – Corso, Ferlinghetti and Ginsberg). The face to be presented bore a stark white complexion emphasised by very dark eyeliner for the girls

(Below) **A tantalising glimpse into how all the right bits were kept not just in and out, but also up and away.** (Opposite) **Not, rather surrpisingly, a portrait of a blithe young thing with a touch of the vapours caught unawares, but a model in an evening dress (and risible pose).**

Cool Baby

The perfect, high-heeled, pencil-skirted 'sweater girl'. It was 1956, and this justly self-regarding young vision of loveliness had just been crowned 'Queen of Soho'.

and jaw-line beards for the boys, all made extra-meaningful by profound and unsmiling – some would say vacuous and bleeding miserable – yearning and soulful glances, spiked by the odd squint of insight. Black polo-neck sweaters and – for the de Beauvoir to our Sartre – equally black opaque stockings and high-heeled shoes were just about essential, as was the mouth-dangled cigarette, the blue veil of smoke for peering through. The cigarette, of course, was more or less vital for everyone, the particular brand betraying who or what you thought you were: du Maurier for would-be sophisticates, anything soft-packed and American for the Jimmy Dean crowd, Gauloises for 'Outsiders' and the beatnik intellectuals, Three Castles and Passing Clouds for the posh nobs, Craven 'A' for the mums ('Will Not Affect Your Throat'), Players for Dad, Woodbine for the workers and roll-ups for the broke.

Many young women, however, very much favoured the dressier and shapelier look. French and Italian influences were everywhere, oomphily combining the allure of two very big (in just about all senses) film stars of the period – the Latin Gina Lollobrigida, and that original and definitive Fifties

sex kitten, St Brigitte of St Tropez. Women were still very proud of the fact that their figures went out, and then they went in (and nor were men too visibly depressed by this state of affairs) and it would have been hard at this time to even foresee, let alone comprehend, the coming appeal of Twiggy's malnutritious waif, ten years on.

The look was achieved by means of a roll-on garment (less constraining than a pre-war corset, but still, I am told, no picnic) and a jutting and conically wired bra, cunningly designed to give pertness to one's points. A suspender belt

The older generation just didn't see the point.

The glamourpuss
is in leopardskin –
and snuggling up
to a frankly terrified
Sabrina (what a
trooper this
bombshell was – a
pro to her fingertips).

(Opposite) **All sorts
of terribly madly
gay examples of
'Loveliness by Post',
all of which, in the
eyes of a teenage
chick, were naturally
to be avoided by
anyone less than a
hundred years old.**

and a pair of the new sheer 'nylons' (be still my beating heart) completed the deal. When form-fitting knitwear was added to the whole, the resultant vision of loveliness was referred to as a 'sweater girl', as exemplified in the rather cheeky pin-up cartoons in the jaunty and cavalier men's magazines of the day. Vargas, in the newly-launched *Playboy*, was the undisputed king of the genre, but infinite variations on the theme could be found and ogled in such esteemed if saucy periodicals as *Lilliput*, *Knave*, *Mister*, *Spick* and (yes) *Span*. The skirt would have been a pencil line, the vertiginous shoes in the earlier part of the decade still sporting that slight clunkiness of Forties designs – in complete contrast with the kitten-heeled winklepickers of 1959. They were all the rage for girls (and, later, boys too) – and so it wasn't long, predictably, before not just chiropodists but spoilsports, prudes and other assorted miseryguts joined forces to condemn the style as being anything from, variously, a crusher of bones to the undiluted work of Satan. Needless to say, no fashion-conscious young thing gave a damn about that, and broad smiles were the order of the day as everyone from debs to shopgirls quite happily click-clacked along from Dolcis to the Odeon.

Look – girls just want to have *fun*, OK? What they were sick to death with from childhood onwards was being forced into stuff that made them look like shrunken versions of their mothers. And although the whole revolution would not be complete until the mid-Sixties, courtesy of Mary Quant, at least now there was scope to enable the cool-conscious chick to avoid as if contaminated anything that remotely smacked of a two-piece 'costume', two-tone court shoes and matching handbag, toning gloves (one worn, one held), pearls, furs and

printed frocks (and particularly any example that had actually been knocked up by one's well-meaning mother from a Flair or Simplicity pattern, and will be absolutely *heavenly*, she would breathlessly insist, for warm afternoons in the *garden*). Girls didn't want to spend warm afternoons in the garden, did they? They wanted to squander them, oh – just anywhere else in the world, if they were honest, and preferably with a boy who had a car or a motorbike or a Vespa or Lambretta scooter so that they could get wherever as fast as possible. Wheels were just the coolest thing because then just the two of you could be alone and together, yet thrill to being in the midst of a getaway – and sometimes, down some lonely twilit lane, at the golden verge of a cornfield or even (beggars can't be choosers, let's face it) up an alley or stuck in the garage, such cosy intimacies could rapidly result in what easily passed in the dark for *luuuurve*.

(Below) **The Chevrolet Impala here is at the 1959 Earl's Court Motor Show – with a girl with a face like the back of a car.** *(Opposite)* **Sex on two wheels in the form of the 'sweater girl' to end all sweater girls: one more bombshell, and this time Jayne Mansfield.**

Jayne Mansfield

Lambretta

INNOCENTI

4 A Teenager in Love

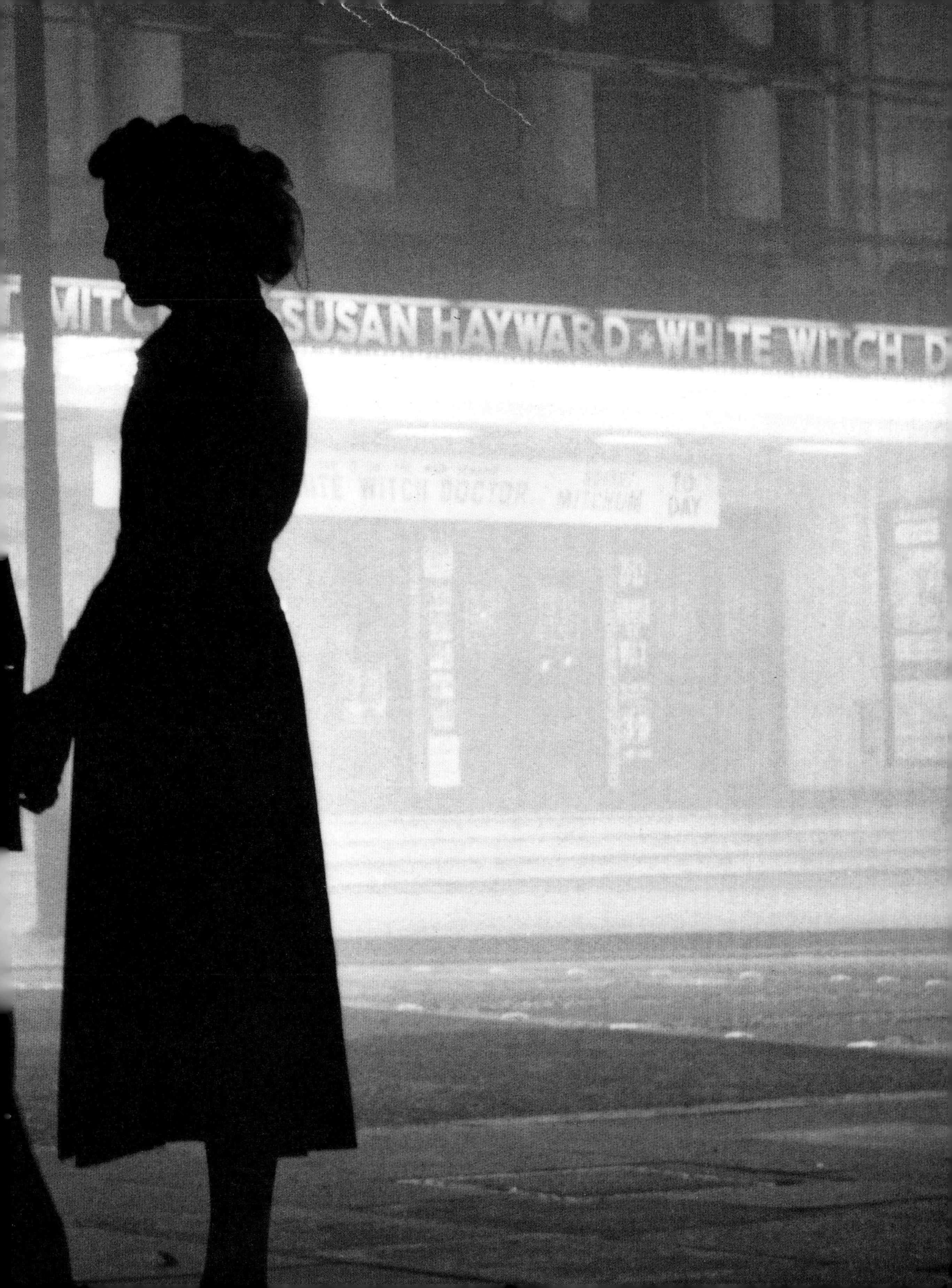
SUSAN HAYWARD
WITCH DOCTOR
MITCHUM

All those gorgeous and gooey pop songs: you are Only Sixteen (Craig Douglas) and just yearn to mumble Sweet Nothin's (Brenda Lee) into the ear of your own Dream Lover (Bobby Darin) and all the while – courtesy of a cadged Kensitas – Smoke Gets in Your Eyes (The Platters). What a Stupid Cupid! (Connie Francis).

The clean-cut American image *(opposite)*, and our version *(above)* – the legendary 2 Is coffee bar in London's Soho.

ook – what with school ('Must try harder') and National Service ('You 'orrible shower!') and mad old parents who kept their daughters locked up in chains, for many young men the idea of a real live girl, to have and to hold, was little more than a fanciful rumour, endlessly doing the rounds. I mean yes, OK – one was aware of the anatomical differences (largely due to sisters, and so forth – though admittedly some of the finer points were still on the hazy side) but could they *really* be, girls, persuaded to – you know, come out and share a coffee, maybe? A Coke and a hot dog (bit pricey, but think of it as an investment)? Well according to American *films* they were, yes – but then just take one look at American schools! They were co-ed in a way that ours were very much not. In senior year, kids 'hung out' during 'recess' – boys and girls, cool-looking and sun-tanned, flirting like

crazy and making really proper and grown-up 'dates' to go bowling or to grab themselves a burger and fries in some lemon and pink soda drugstore glittering with chrome with a benevolent proprietor called something like Doc or Pop – and then maybe take in a drive-in in the old man's Chevvy! I mean – good

grief! What *we* did was skulk about the toilets in the rainy playground, all lads together, sucking surreptitiously on a quite vile Woodbine and passing from hand to hand a much-riffled and practically archival copy of (rude) *Health and Efficiency* (the air-brushed bits in the photos only serving to fuel the mounting pyre of our bamboozlement: how could such seamlessness just there – and there! – be at all possible? Here indeed may well have been health – but God alone knew where efficiency entered; or, come to that, anything else).

So what we needed, and fast,

Just one of the many American options. We got our burgers from Bird's Eye or the Wimpy Bar (and, for that matter, our dogs from Battersea, but this is maybe not what is meant here).

were all the props we could get – and pre-eminent among them was a guitar. Some clever dicks actually went so far as to take lessons, but initially this was seen to be missing the point, big time: you hung it around your neck and posed and mimed in front of the mirror (strumming that Slazenger became a thing of the past). Wear it in public, and the girls would saunter on over (although it has to be said that guys would snigger – and if you didn't have a single chord to your name, you were heading for a drubbing; it was at this stage that many Bert Weedon books were sold).

Ten-pin bowling in Milwaukee, in all the right gear. And afterwards? How about one of Fifties America's peerless and open-all-hours drugstores, a glorious example of which is seen overleaf: buy some shades, maybe, name your soda, sit up high on a barstool with your girl and just be cool, man.

But everything seemed so much easier in America – kids over there all seemed to have such a lot of time and money and clothes and opportunities (according to imported Harvey Comics and the pictures, anyway – the nearest to the States any of us was likely to get). 'Dad!' we could hear repeatedly and with mounting exasperation. 'OK if I borrow the car tonight?' OK if I borrow the *car* tonight?! In this country – always assuming that our father even ran to something on the lines of a Standard Vanguard or a Vauxhall Victor or a Hillman Minx or a Singer Gazelle, he would be as likely to lend it to us as to

A Teenager in Love

After the prom was over ... maybe grab some milk and gaze up at the light of the moon (helped out by neon).

(Opposite)
Unspeakably enviable – American kids in a customised hot-rod and *(overleaf)* the sort of place they well might go to.

set about the thing with an axe and chain-saw: he might have seen his way to grudgingly extending you a ten-bob note, but that he'd want back by Friday, latest. And worse – more often than not, these damn young Yankees seemed to have their *own* set of wheels – and not in the form of the clapped-out third-hand creaking Ford Popular that we might just about have managed (if we'd come up lucky with a fifty-pound Premium Bond prize from good old Ernie, say, or else robbed the Bank of England). Our transatlantic cousins drove customised old-style two-tone hot-rods, the windshields and aerials streaming with campus pennants and rainbow-coloured pom-poms. Why pom-poms? Because there'd be no trouble, would there, in a car like that, in laying claim and then siege to yet one more example of what seemed wholly designed to drive the pale and not-too-interesting British boy wild with wonder and desire: a *cheerleader*! (Give it an 'L', give it a 'U', give it an 'S' – and let's all hear it for a 'T'! Yay!) It just wasn't going to happen, was it, if the latter part of the evening was spent poring over a grime-edged and much-unfolded timetable, in order to check up again on that truly terrible thing: the last bus home (and redolent, it would be, of not just stale fag-ash, but also lost opportunities). *They* had drive-in coffee shops the size and luminescence of an A40 service station; we had coffee shops so damn small that you had to queue for ever just by the coats with trellised ivy and a knackered cheese plant nuzzling one's ear in the vain hope of one of those weeny triangular tables, each of which was smugly colonised by on-the-ball couples so well versed in the art of eking out a pair of one-and-fourpenny cappuccinos until – well, until the time

"2·4·6·8...WHAT DO WE APPRECIATE?" FOOD AND THIS

fresh, clean taste!

Nothing does it like Seven-Up

Those cheers you hear *after* the game are for something-to-eat and 7-Up! The fans say that when you have 7-Up, the hamburgers taste meatier, the hot dogs taste zestier, and French fries taste more like French fries than ever. (What they mean is that 7-Up between bites wakes up your taste buds so you can taste *all* the good food flavors.) See for yourself what the shouting's about! YOU LIKE IT...IT LIKES YOU

(Opposite) **An *English* couple, believe it or not, though clearly smitten by all things transatlantic. Even the Coke bottles are authentic – and the Buick is just about the very last word.**

The sort of Saturday night get-together that made the whole of the rest of the week worthwhile.

came to scramble for the last sodding bus home (and how these coffee bars ever made money was truly a mystery to everyone).

The basic difference appeared to be that America would actually encourage an integrated young male and female society, whereas over here we seemed destined to longingly peer across the chasmic divide, occasionally exchanging a postcard. *They* had high school proms where the boy would get all togged up in a white tuxedo with a red carnation and he'd call for his party-frocked date and present her with a toning corsage. A fairly grisly concept, admittedly – but all we on the other hand had were clunky school dances where moody boys would cluster on the one side and glare inscrutably at the massed ranks of girls, all rustling and giggling, on the other – sipping through straws and, though yearning to dance, affecting indifference and even contempt with such chilling conviction as to deter any young man from so much as even chancing it. Because if you were to swallow hard and walk the endless walk and pipingly come up with 'Care To Dance?' (with just the one voice break in the middle) there could only, couldn't there, be one of two responses coming in your direction? And despite those notional odds of fifty-fifty, the risk was quite simply too great.

So what you had to do was get a girl alone – but how? And – more to the point – where? Going back to her (or your) place was pretty much a no-no due to those perpetual irritants, mothers and fathers (not to say bleeding inquisitive younger brothers). Hence the popularity of bracing country walks,

(Opposite) **An American barbecue, pumped up by the bounce of Pepsi.** (Below) **A different sort of bubbles (only slightly more potent). 'I'd love a Babycham' was, for a time, just about the most sophisticated, sexy (and expensive) thing a girl could utter.**

deserted beaches, London parks in the summer (or, let's face it, through hail and snow – when you're hungry, you'll eat anywhere). Good too was any sort of cubbyhole under the stairs if one were fortunate enough to have been asked to what passed for a party. These 'parties' were humble affairs – Smith's Crisps, radishes, Suncrush, a drop of Watney's Pale Ale or Double Diamond (maybe Babycham, if pushing out the boat was on the agenda), Cliff on the Dansette and – oh my God – home by eleven, my girl (or else). The difficulty with sex in the Fifties was fundamentally this: everyone knew that nice girls just *didn't* – whereas boys (whether nice, not nice, or out-and-out repellent) could think of little else – apart from, of course, those eternal exceptions: football, beer, guitars and spots. Cuddles, gropes and kisses, then, were all kindly bestowed and eagerly received – but it was this place called 'All The Way' where every boy yearned to go, though where was the clear and signposted A-route? It often came down to a long and winding journey down unmade lanes with plenty of stops in lay-bys and long red lights at major junctions, only to discover much later that all the time they had been puttering along the ring road, the town centre having been somehow, yet again, bypassed altogether.

I'd love a Babycham

the happiest drink in the world
BABYCHAM

The Babycham bottle fills a champagne glass

FUN'S-A-COOKIN'—WITH PLENTY OF PEPSI!
More Bounce to the Ounce
Pepsi-Cola
Pepsi-Cola
Drink Pepsi-Cola
Why take less ... when Pepsi's best!
On Television see Faye Emerson weekly over CBS-TV—
On Radio hear Phil Regan weekly over CBS

But then, for the lucky ones, would come that big real thing called (gurgle it low) *luuuurve*, baby – at long last, a sweet romance. Holidays, of course, were simply the greatest times – all constraints just blown away, money in one's pocket, precious little time and a determination to wring out of it all the goodness going. A few of the pluckier ones might be, goodness me, 'jetting off' to

A Teenager in Love

this place called 'Abroad' on BEA or even via a BOAC 'Speedbird World Air Route' (the Spanish packages cranked up in 1959 – anyone for fifteen days in Majorca at just forty-four guineas?). The majority of us, though, would be off to Bournemouth, Scarborough, Blackpool, Broadstairs – or maybe to one of the booming Butlin's holiday camps, where even if such impedimenta as parents and siblings were in tow, it was fairly easy to slope off in quest of rapture.

And when it happened, oh boy – you knew it all right: everything you'd always heard and read

The sight of the sun in her hair, and the smell of the dew on the grass ...

about now sprang up in front of your eyes, live and fully formed: the meeting of a glance, that scintillating sparkle of just *something* – a soft caress of sun-warmed shoulders set against the sudden tingle of a large size Lyons Maid Raspberry Ripple (digging in alternately with just the one shared wooden spatula) as dark and longing eyes are mutually gazed at and deeply into. And, says with defiance the teenager in love, this *isn't*, actually, merely some holiday romance, just another summer thing – because look: we've exchanged home addresses and we're going to write to each other every single day and maybe even twice on Sundays and we've taken pictures with the Brownie which we'll keep in a box in a drawer with our very most secret things and we'll play and play our special record and love one another for ever and a day, or until we die, whichever comes first. *Kiss* me, sweetheart – and hold me tight, yes? Because we're both going home tomorrow ... and I so don't want to leave you.

(Opposite)
... Sights and smells of a different order – but who was to know just when and how love would come and tap you on the shoulder? These two deserve their pocketful of starlight.

5 Move It

Rock 'n' roll: the driving beat at the heart of the Fifties – a clarion call that jangled our nerve-ends, and touched and then vanquished our collective soul. And when we came to hit the dancefloor – oh boy! It electrified your feet and rattled your brain: A whole *lot* of shakin' goin' on ...

Entering into the spirit of the thing: swept off her feet, and loving every moment.

Going to the pictures was one thing – all well and good, and a rare chance to get to know one another better at the back of the stalls. But when the hormones and energy levels were charging all through you (and when, let's face it, were they not?) then some outlet more direct and immediate was urgently called for, and there was only one place to go: the Mecca, the Palais de Danse – the room above the dicey pub with a dais at one end for the beery band, the draughty scout hut or even the mildewed village hall. Decor and style were hardly the key, here: all we wanted to know was, could the music keep on coming till we dropped down damp, exhausted and pleasured beyond belief? Because that's what we needed – here and now, we just had to rip it up.

Is they is, or is they ain't? Yes they am.

And – as is so often true when special delights are occasional and treasured – the tingle of anticipation was so much a part. The scanning of those luridly fluorescent and hand-painted posters throughout the week, touting such as the Empire Ballroom (capacity 193: *must* be vacated by 11 pm, prompt) where no

Look, it's five-thirty in the morning on a cold January day in 1959, close to the end of an all-night carnival of jazz at the Albert Hall – so I think you'll agree a little understanding is in order.

less than So-and-So and the So-and-Sos would be billed as being *that* close to a recording deal with Decca or Columbia! Either that or the band from the local youth club was up for it (if they could just lay their hands on some skins) and rehearsing like crazy the finer points of those scarce imported American 78s and 45s (deforming the vowels and coaxing the lips into a drive-'em-wild and look-at-me-I'm-Elvis sneer, while getting those knees to tremble and shake).

And then there was all the vital palaver of Getting Ready – very much the girl's preserve, this protracted ritual, as any mother could have despairingly told you: 'When are you going to help me with the ironing?': 'Can't, Mum – getting ready.' 'Can you quickly slip down to the shops, then? We're out of Omo and your father wants fish fingers for his supper.': 'You do it, Mum – I've got to get *ready*.': 'Well at least come down and eat your Munchmallow, then – your tea's getting cold.': 'Do it *later*, Mum, OK? Getting *ready*.'

And nor was she kidding – preparation for the Saturday night out on the town would start not much later than early afternoon. First she had to see to the liberal application of Immac to all sorts of areas that boys would come to be stunned to learn were not in fact naturally smooth and free of darkish down – and then came the all-important business of her *official* hair. If she had spent all morning at the hairdresser (clutching a shot of Marilyn Monroe clipped from that month's *Picturegoer*: 'I want it like *that* …') then it was a matter of

About as cool and rocky as it gets. This is actually a sequence from the 1959 film *Serious Charge*, which also featured Cliff Richard.

carefully inserting the stiffly hairsprayed whole into a ruched and vile-smelling shower cap in order to protect it while bathing. Otherwise it was out with not just Silvikrin or Drene but also the Twink or Toni curling kits, or maybe even the tear-making fierceness of lethal peroxide (all things were placidly endured if shimmering platinum were the promised outcome – the reality often more akin, it must be said, to a scarecrow's protrusions), or else the unalloyed terror that was part and parcel of colouring: entering into the unknown with only a bottle of traitorous henna to see you through. The bath itself (Did anyone put the tank on? Well who's pinched all the hot water, then?) involved a generous scattering of birthday-present Goya bath salts, maybe (Can't stand Dad's Radox) and a languorous lathering of 'fabulous pink Camay' – in order to bolster the ongoing process of becoming just 'a little lovelier each day'. Careful attention was paid with the Odo-ro-no and then a vigorous brushing with Pepsodent (wondering the while just where the yellow went; can't stand Dad's Gibbs'

When a form-fitting dress comes out a winner over one of those circular, petticoated skirts just made for dancing. Or not, depending on your point of view.

Dentifrice). After that it was down to checking that good old Mum and Robin Starch had jointly worked their magic on all those crunkled petticoats, and then the studied unfurling of either Bear Brand or Ballito nylons in Dark Mink or Flesh, according to not just taste, but intent. Now for a touch of Outdoor Girl rouge, scarlet Rimmel lipstick and lashings of well-spittled mascara. And what of the boy? A basin and a bar of Lifebuoy will do him, followed by twenty minutes horsing around with comb and Brylcreem and then he's off (and just you try and stop him).

And the best of the dancing was wild: the one linked hand of the great Fifties jive afforded the swingers all sorts of configurations – spinning and reeling and hurling the girl right up and over your back and round and down again, if you truly felt up to it. These damn thick brothel-creepers were bouncing to the beat, layered skirts were flying high – and if a bass sax was there too to honk out those rudest of raspberries, the blood pulsated all the more joyously. '*Move* it', exhorted Cliff Richard in his first and possibly finest single – and

Night-time fun at the fair: take in the pulsating rock, clanking buffers and bells, the shimmer of lights – and just hang loose and wait for action.

the kids on the floor didn't need to be told: they would be out there kicking, reeling and a-rocking for ever and ever – eager to go for it all around the clock. And the music followed you to fun fairs, too – other cool places with thrilling rides where the guy would quell his nausea and do his best to be brave and the

Wherever you just happen to be is surely the place to rock – *(above)* an impromptu jive in a Soho square, and *(opposite)* some serious jitterbugging on a New York rooftop.

girl could scream out loud and those fabulous skirts would take life again and tantalise you nearly to death. Fairgrounds were wonderful places for boys and girls to legitimately mingle – and, unlike so much in Britain, they were open at night. It was OK to be seen doing silly, throwback, childish things (great things, therefore) like making one's whole face pink and sticky as a result of tackling a cloud of candy floss in the face of a gale, or taking potshots at a trundling line of tin-plate ducks and winning for the girl a straw-stuffed Kewpie doll or one of those singular inflatable picaninnies, replete with dangling loop earrings. You could hurl a plywood hoop at a great glass jar of Pascall Fruit Bonbons with a real five-pound note and a could-be gold watch elastic-banded around its girth – and the hoop would encircle it to whoops of triumph and then dumbly lodge on the wooden plinth: never mind, mate – here, have a goldfish in a polythene bag. Blow that – let's catch up with the raucous sounds and have another ride.

The music never left you – it was in your head and on the streets and piped out tinnily on Radio Luxembourg from your pocket transistor. Whenever and wherever young people met, music would somehow be made – tea chests, washboards, galvanised bins, milk bottles and oil drums were all pressed into urgent service – and then the jive could get up and going. Dance on, as the man said – and yeah, that's just what we're gonna do.

And if no band was around? Well then head for the more clued-up dance halls – those coffee bars that make the others look like not much more than a

chain-store tea shop: head for those that boast the ultimate – a juke box. Connie Francis sang to us all about how she dreamed of a Robot Man because unlike a real live man, who'd give her grief (always make her cry into her handkerchief), she could, you see, *depend* upon a robot love. But for most of us the robot of choice would have been the Wurlitzer – a seemingly miraculous and so hot and alluring great friendly machine that would at the touch of a button (and yes, OK – the insertion of a tanner) play you any record in the world that you wanted to hear – and if you had a crush or a pash on the platter of the moment or just felt in the mood for hogging the whole scene, it would happily spin the thing again and again. Now. Be honest: was this not very heaven? Even the sight of the selector through the lit-up window, extend-

(Below) **The mighty juke box! Just gazing at the thing was a joy in itself.** *(Opposite)* **The absolute last word – the classic Wurlitzer, in all its gaudy glory.**

ing in its own time a leisurely arm and planking down on the turntable the vinyl of choice with the huge central hole – it gripped you with a sense of awe and wonder.

And it is no surprise at all that authentic Fifties rockers who all these years on are now quite grown up (well – not *really*) often spring for the original version so that they can rock along to the same old sounds – and so what if they're now a little bit crackly? The thump of the beat and the twanging guitars go on blaring right at you: the spirit of the thing – like the Wurlitzer itself – continues to gleam.

Musicals reached their zenith during the Fifties – *Oklahoma!*, *Carmen Jones*, *Singin' in the Rain*,

"Oh Boy, they have WURLITZER MUSIC!"

America's favorite nickel's worth of fun

All over America today, people in search of good entertainment at a reasonable price are learning to look for the Wurlitzer *Sign of the Musical Note*.

There you find Wurlitzer Music . . . 24 of the latest tunes played by the greatest bands in the land . . . for only a nickel a number. Pick your favorites from a musical menu of sweet numbers, jazz classics, hill billy hits, waltzes, fox trots, polkas.

You'll go home humming their haunting melodies, higher in spirit, happier at heart for having spent a pleasant musical interlude by spending only a few small coins. That's why Wurlitzer Music is nationally known as *America's Favorite Nickel's Worth of Fun*. The Rudolph Wurlitzer Company, North Tonawanda, New York.

The *Sign of the Musical Note* identifies places where you can have fun playing a Wurlitzer.

THE NAME THAT MEANS *Music* **TO MILLIONS**

The music of Wurlitzer pianos, accordions, electronic organs, and juke boxes is heard "'round the world." Wurlitzer is America's largest manufacturer of pianos all produced under one name . . . also America's largest, best known manufacturer of juke boxes and accordions.

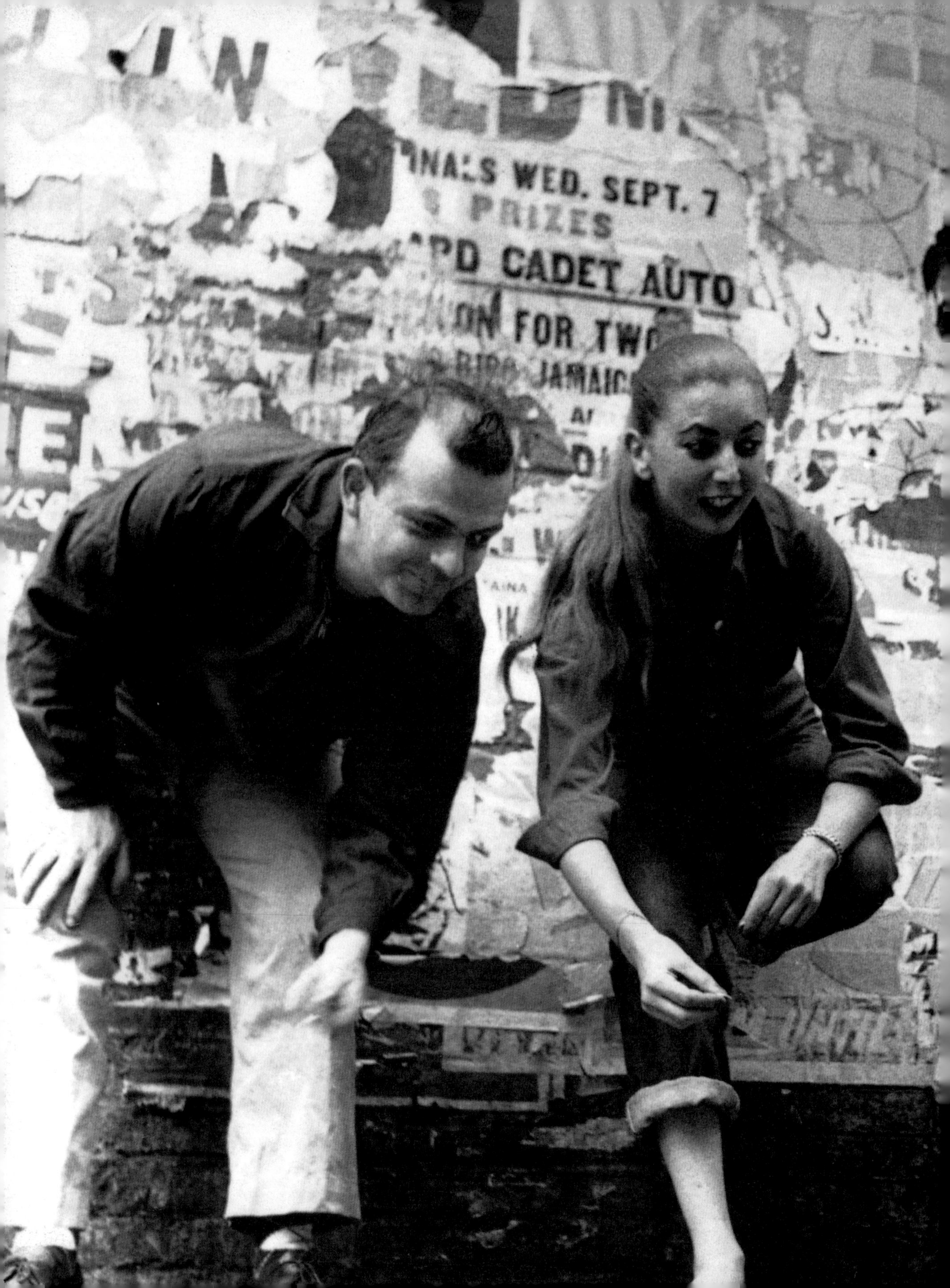
INALS WED. SEPT. 7
PRIZES
PD CADET AUTO
ON FOR TWO

AMUSEMENT PARK N.J.
DIRECT BUSES FROM N.Y.C.
SURF BATHING
SALT WATER POOL
FUN
WORLD'S LARGEST
KIDDIE PARK
20 RIDES
ALSO
FREE
PARKING
DANCING

**(Previous pages)
Getting on down in
New York City and
(above) the more
sedate London version
(when you stop to look
at it, the hand jive *was*
kinda crazy, wasn't it?)**

Seven Brides for Seven Brothers, South Pacific, Guys and Dolls – and none more influential or capturing more perfectly the zeitgeist than the original stage production of Bernstein and Sondheim's *West Side Story* (the film didn't come till 1961). This opened the floodgates for not just would-be hoofers auditioning for any amateur production of any musical going, but also a huge and visible boom in syncopated ambling, whistling low and the snapping of fingers ('Cool it boy, Crazy boy …'): for many at the time, the most beautiful sound they had ever heard.

So – the temperature was up, rock was on a roll – and all in all it was driving the oldies crazy with trumped-up outrage, barely veiled jealousy and quite possibly genuine migraines (always a very healthy state of affairs). But they would get their revenge whenever one of the very occasional pop programmes appeared on television. *Oh Boy!* – or Jack Good's *Six-Five Special* ('clickety-clack, clickety-clack …') – and *parents*

Carve yourself a piece of the action – before it's time to kick the bucket.

wanted to watch the, oh God – news and *weather* (can you believe it?) or *Emergency Ward Ten* or even Fanny and Johnnie Craddock (always assuming they were in the mood to neither take their pick nor double their money), and in a pitilessly hierarchical set-up like home there was simply no way round this except to rapidly decamp to some other TV-owning household with more enlightened custodians (or, to put it another way, other people's parents who had just popped round the corner or were outside clipping the privet or had recently *died*, or something). But why why why on earth couldn't any of them understand how terribly *important* it was?

Phew. All hot and bothered, now. Think I'll just sit this one out … hey! Why don't we do that crazy hand jive? What's that you say? Turn down the volume and just sit *still*? Yeah, sure, right: *that'll* be the day.

6

Rave On

The greatest times for all worshippers at the altars of their choice were those never-to-be-forgotten moments when they actually could come within breathing distance – almost, so nearly, reach out and touch – their very own gods. Those black-and-white TV midgets now became full-size, and colour. This, to a fan, was simply the best.

While Elvis *(previous pages)* **wows them, Cliff keeps his distance (wise, if you look at them: lusty, very).**

Elvis, of course, was the king of kings – everyone who caught his debut single 'Heartbreak Hotel' in 1956 seems in retrospect to have either lathered themselves up into an unstoppable frenzy, or else were

Tommy Steele –
Britain's first home-
grown rocker – lost
to the world, and
really going for it.

just felled by the sort of faint that left them for dead. But our own home-grown
cheeky chappie Tommy Steele actually beat Elvis to the British Number One spot
by a good six months with 'Singing the Blues' (the King's first number one over
here was, appropriately, 'All Shook Up', in 1957). And four months later, twenty-
year-old Tommy was, um, filming his life story and reportedly earning six
hundred pounds a week (at a time when many of us felt convinced that we
would never amass dough of that order during the cumulative whole of the rest
of our lives). Cliff, meanwhile, was rapidly dubbed the English Elvis (cool cat
quiff, moody eyes and crooked lips) and by 1959 seemed to have the entire nation
in thrall with such eminently hummable ditties as 'Living Doll' and 'Travellin'
Light' – both of them number one hits, to be sure, but neither in the league of his
down-and-dirty debut, 'Move It'; America never saw the point of Cliff.

Rave On

In between breathless bouts of rock, we still had time for the traditional balladeers – most of us recall sharing those Magic Moments with Perry Como, and nor will we forget our debt of gratitude to Dean Martin for mellowly putting a name to just what that thing is when the moon hits our eye like a big pizza pie ('That's Amore'). But the boss was fellow ratpacker Sinatra, who made us all want to pack up those bags and fly away – to *Chic*-ago (look – if it's Frank's kinda town, then it's sure as hell good enough for me) and also to discover as a matter of some urgency just how it might

An unlikely trio, on the face of it: the three chief members of the ratpack – Sammy Davis Jnr *(above left),* **Dean Martin** *(above right)* **and** *(opposite)* **the epitome of cool, Mister Frank Sinatra.**

feel to be – or have – a 'Swinging Lover' (which sounded good from where we were standing).

Rock 'n' roll, though, would always be the driving force. Bill Haley and the Comets simply drove audiences wild – with the exception of Sinatra, in the Forties, the first real signs of fan hysteria (which is odd, when you look at them). Similarly frenzied receptions were accorded to the extraordinary crooner Johnnie Ray, whose act consisted of a good deal of jerking about like

(Opposite)
**Lonnie Donegan,
signing photos and
being Quasimodo.
Or maybe he's just
feeling the cold.**

a thing possessed, throttling the living daylights out of the microphone stand
before slithering on down it and then, while practically prostrate, crying his
eyes out. This last reduced his thousands of female fans to helplessness and
tears: so not a dry eye in the house, then.

When Haley brought his Comets to London in 1957, he simply wowed us.
As far as we were concerned, being repeatedly exhorted to Shake, Rattle and
Roll (not to say Razzle Dazzle) was really no more than very good advice
indeed, and we lost no time in putting the plan into action. Elvis, though, – to
the lasting disappointment of his legions of adorers – never ever made it to
Britain: shame – he (and we) would really have loved it. Still – we had his elec-
trifying performance in *Jailhouse Rock* to warm us, and the rude exuberance

**Bill Haley and one
of his Comets get
momentarily legless.**

of 'Hound Dog', 'Blue Suede Shoes' and 'Party' reminded us (huh! – as if we needed reminding) that we all still Gotta Lot o' Livin' To Do.

Another huge American star was he of the trademark square-framed specs, Buddy Holly (and his Crickets); it was Buddy, before his tragically early death at the age of twenty-three, who told us to Rave On – so we did. And guess what? In so many ways, we're raving still – and never more so than when we wallow in the recall of that very special thrill that only a live performance could send rippling right through you. The 'king of skiffle', Lonnie Donegan, was particularly good value – his increasingly fast and furious gui-

A still from the 1959 film *Expresso Bongo* featuring Cliff Richard, here seen not being Hank Marvin.

(*Previous pages*) Johnnie Ray's English fan club gathers to welcome him to Heathrow airport. He asked them all back to the Dorchester Hotel and gave them each a glass of fizzy lemonade. Which is nice.

tar-playing allied to the warbled crescendo of his tirelessly quite frantic voice could get them rocking in the aisles like nobody's business ('Don't You Rock Me Daddy-O' – I can do it all alone). Number one hits such as 'Cumberland Gap', which – then as now – you either love or hate, drew attention to not just Donegan's prowess on the guitar, but to the instrument itself. It was no longer OK in the eyes of the fans for a star to have just any old guitar slung around his neck: they were now into brands, and could detect with ease all the nuances.

In Britain, it was largely down to Hank Marvin's elegant footwork and – more to the point – his constant twiddling of this endlessly fascinating chromi-

um lever at the base of his guitar that made so many young men swoon and yearn to possess one of these sleek and solid-bodied electrical marvels. The definitive Fifties guitar has to be the legendary Fender Stratocaster, the much imitated organic design being quite revolutionary and very sexy at the time (and, as we know, no less so now). The Strat – much favoured by Buddy Holly – cost two hundred and fifty dollars as early as 1954, so you more or less had to be Buddy Holly to have a hope of affording one. The Gretsch was the choice of Eddie Cochran, Chet Atkins and Bo Diddley (increasingly brightly coloured and weirdly shaped – the guitars, that is), while the Gibson Les Paul

– and in particular the 'gold top' model – was very much prized by those in the know (despite irresistible word association in this country with a United Dairies full-cream Jersey pinta).

We, in our rooms at home, would have settled for any one of them. Or even one of the mail order knock-offs that merely bore a passing resemblance (didn't matter anyway, as we were wholly unlikely to be able to actually *play* the thing); yes, they were cheap but, alas – as was so often the way – not cheap enough. What we could (just about) afford, however, were records: records were heaven – records were what kept us sane when we were all alone, and pining for more. On a Saturday morning, we knew exactly which single, EP or (if it was something of a red letter day) even LP we were going to buy because of course we had plotted and saved for it and thought of little else for the better

part of the week. There was no harm at all in listening to three or four others in the shop, though – all very exciting. You held what looked like an elongated telephone receiver close to your ear and concentrated hard upon the blend of crackle, hiss and record shop hubbub which was all that ever came over; often you got to hear a good deal of the record being played in the booth next door, though, whether or not you wanted to.

Back home fast, and straight up to your room. Take Paul Anka's 'Diana' off the turntable, give the new

This very strange lady seems to think her rather smart portable is something more on the lines of a musical box – and maybe, judging by the gloves, contaminated to boot.

Lite is sweeter with a

Dansette
the truest name in sound

Made in England

BERMUDA
16½ gns. tax paid

The only set at its price to offer you all these latest design features: new BSR 4-speed changer, quality amplifier giving rich full-range reproduction, genuine diamond needle, sockets for stereo, tape and extension speakers—plus many more new features. Legs optional 2 gns extra.

See these Dansettes at your dealer, or send for colour brochure of the full range – 26 Dansettes.

GEM
the most popular portable transistor!
11½ gns tax paid

22 gns.

CONSORT
Greatest value in tape recorders! Light, elegant, compact—the portable with everything you want. Gives up to 1½ hours playing time per reel, and records from microphone, gramophone or radio. Quality reproduction, magic eye, independent tone, volume and dub-in controls. Complete with microphone and other accessories.

DANSETTE PRODUCTS LIMITED, DANSETTE HOUSE,

HONEYPOT LANE, STANMORE, MIDDLESEX

The stuff of our dreams, and just how much moolah would have to be raised.

(Overleaf)
Tommy Steele demonstrates with enviable cool just how to go about being a rock star. But just close your eyes, and you can be one too ...

record a careful wiping with a strange little cylinder covered in supposedly anti-static velveteen, clunk on the automatic feeder, and your blue-and-cream Dansette will cope with the rest. And when the record is done? Play the B-side, hate it, and play the A-side again. And again. And again. Repeat until somebody bangs on the wall, and concede with reluctance that it's maybe time to spin an alternative platter. Flick through the black wire record rack with little red ball-end feet and strew around you all the flimsy sleeves – Columbia, London, HMV, Decca, Brunswick, Parlophone, Capitol – as well as the glossy and treasured LPs, some with pinholes in the corners from when you thought that having them over your bed was a good idea. Play them all, and play them loud. Close your eyes and you can be just anyone and anywhere in the world you desire ... the music will do this for you.

And the beat goes on.

Credits

Picture credits are given in source order.

The Advertising Archive: 31, 49, 65, 71, 73, 83, 88, 89, 90, 105, 123

Corbis/Bettmann: 9, 18, 25, 45, 57, 64, 103, 115

Hulton Getty: 2/3, 7, 8, 10, 11, 12, 13, 14/15, 16, 17, 19, 20, 21, 22/23, 26/27, 28, 29, 30, 32/33, 34, 35, 36, 37, 38, 39, 40/41, 42, 43, 44, 46, 47, 48, 50/51, 53, 54, 55, 56, 58, 59, 60, 61, 62, 63, 66, 67, 68, 69, 70, 72, 74/75, 76, 77, 78, 79, 80/81, 82, 84/85, 86, 87, 91, 92, 93, 94/95, 96, 97, 98, 99, 100, 101, 102, 104, 106/107, 108, 109, 112, 113, 116, 117, 118/119, 121, 122, 124/125

Redferns: Glen A. Baker Archives 110/111, 114/Bob Willoughby 114

Acknowledgements

Thanks for the concept are due to commissioning editor Margaret ('Cool Baby') Little. Steve Guise: for not ripping it up. Great thanks also due, as ever, to Steve Cox, copy editor supreme.